Mr. Lincoln's Boys

Being the MOSTLY True Adventures of

Abraham Lincoln's Trouble-Making Sons,

TAD and WILLIE

Mr. Lincoln's Boys

Being the **MOSTLY** True Adventures of

Abraham Lincoln's Trouble-Making Sons,

TAD and WILLIE

By
STATON RABIN

Illustrated by
BAGRAM IBATOULLINE

SCHOLASTIC INC.
New York Toronto London Auckland
Sydney Mexico City New Delhi Hong Kong

Dedicated to the heroes of the FDNY—in Tad and Willie's time, and in ours—S.R.

To Joseph Kunin—B.I.

ISBN: 978-0-545-23252-4

12 11 10 9 8 7 6 5 4 3 2 1   10 11 12 13 14 15/0

Printed in the U.S.A.   08

First Scholastic printing, January 2010

Set in Granjon
Book design by Nancy Brennan

One night long ago in the White House, a very little boy was
having a very bad dream.

Tad sat up in bed, clutching his blanket.

"You awake, Willie?" he said, shaking his brother.

"Am now," Willie grumbled. "Go back to sleep, Tad."

But Tad couldn't sleep. So he did what he always did when he
was afraid. He went to his father.

President Lincoln was working late, reading telegrams. He stretched out his long legs under his desk and sighed. Tad scrambled up his father's legs like a monkey climbing a coconut tree. The boy squirmed into his lap.

"I dreamed everybody was fighting each other! Made no difference whether they were friends, even brothers. A war between the North and the South! Do you think that's what my dream means, Pa?" he asked Mr. Lincoln.

"You believe in dreams, Taddie?"

The boy nodded. "Sometimes. Don't you?"

"Sometimes."

"Is there really going to be a war?"

Tad's father was a very busy man. And he was worried, too. But his boys brought a twinkle to his eye.

"I hope not," he said, mussing Tad's hair. "I hope it won't come to that."

But Tad's dream came true, and the country was torn apart by a civil war.

The year 1861 was a strange, sad time to be a boy in Washington, D.C. Northern soldiers were everywhere, guarding the city from invasion by Southern rebels. Some Northern troops even camped at the White House, where the Lincoln family lived.

Colonel Elmer E. Ellsworth's Fire Zouaves, burly firemen from New York who practiced acrobatic military drills, arrived ready to fight for the Union. Wearing fiery red-and-blue uniforms, they marched down Pennsylvania Avenue shouting, "One! Two! Three! Four! Five! Six! Seven! Tiger! Zouave!" Big ugly guns on carts rolled through the streets with a terrible rumbling like thunder.

One day, Tad and Willie were chasing their pet goat on the White House lawn when she stopped in her tracks and pricked up her ears.

"Pa says there's a battle across the river in Virginia,"
Willie said. "Hear that noise like slamming doors, Tad?
That's big cannons going off, you bet!"

Tad shivered.

Soon, Northern soldiers, tired and hungry, dragged themselves back to Washington from the battle. Their eyes stared from mud-streaked faces.

When they heard the crowd's cheers, the men started marching with a spring in their step. But some children's fathers wore bandages and limped, or had to be carried to hospital beds. And other fathers didn't come back at all.

No, it wasn't an easy time to be a boy in Washington, D.C. Especially if you were the president's sons—with your pa carrying the weight of the war on his shoulders like some big old cannonball. Mr. Lincoln's face got a new worry-wrinkle every day. And wherever his sons went, strangers pointed at them.

"I wish they wouldn't stare at us so," Willie said.
"Wasn't there ever a president who had children?"

But Willie and Tad found ways to be ordinary boys. They loved to pull clever pranks. Tad was two years younger, but he was the ringleader. He would dare Willie to do something, and Willie would go along with it. Like the time they rigged all the signal bells in the attic to ring at once. Servants rushed up and down the stairs, wondering who had called them.

Old Edward the doorkeeper opened the door and no one was there. *The bells were bewitched!* Mr. Lincoln's secretaries, John Nicolay and John Hay, ran to the president's office. They feared it was a great national emergency. When they found out the truth, they were furious. But the president just laughed.

People said the Lincoln boys were out of control. Mr. Hay wanted to wring their little necks and toss them out his window. The army officers felt the same way.

Imagine old General So-and-So, trying to talk to the president about troops and provisions and battle plans. And there were Willie and Tad, one on each of Mr. Lincoln's knees. His sons chattered and teased. They bounced up and down like toy

boats. They pinched the president's cheeks and pulled his long nose. They laughed and squealed until the poor old tired general finally said, "Mr. President, can't you *do* something about those rascals?!"

But whenever anyone complained about his sons, Mr. Lincoln just smiled and said, "Let the children have a good time."

Sometimes Tad and Willie played soldier. But to Mr. Lincoln's boys, this was no game—being soldiers was serious business. They wore Zouave uniforms, like the men in their brave friend Colonel Elmer Ellsworth's regiment. Colonel Ellsworth had gotten killed capturing a Rebel flag in Virginia. For the Lincoln boys, wearing the Zouave uniform became one way of remembering him.

Elmer would have been proud of his young friends. They drilled the White House servants like army troops. Willie was the colonel, and Tad was the noisy drum major.

They named themselves "Mrs. Lincoln's Zouaves" and manned a toy cannon on the roof of the White House, keeping a keen eye out for Rebel troops.

"Let 'em come!" said Drum Major Tad. "Willie and I are ready for 'em."

Sometimes Tad took guard duty at the bottom of the grand staircase in the White House. When visitors came to see the president, he blocked their way.

"Halt! Five cents, please," he'd say. "It's for the Sanitary Commission." That was a charity to help soldiers, like today's Red Cross.

Once the visitors paid up, Tad let them pass.

One day, Mrs. Lincoln and her young friend Julia, who often kept an eye on the children, heard off-key music coming through a window at the White House.

"What in heaven's name is that noise, Julia?" Mrs. Lincoln asked.

"It's probably the dead march," she replied. "I suppose the boys are burying Jack again."

Jack was the boys' soldier doll. He wore a tiny Zouave uniform and always seemed to be getting into trouble. One week, they'd catch him spying for the enemy. The next, the boys would accuse him of deserting his post.

Earlier that morning, Willie and Tad had put Jack on trial for the dozenth time.

"You deserve no mercy," Tad had said to Jack in a deep, judge's voice. "I hereby sentence Private Jack to death by firing squad!"

They took Jack outside the White House and propped him against a wall. The boys tied a tiny blindfold on him.

"Ready . . . aim . . ." Tad ordered. They squinted in the bright sun and aimed their cannon at Jack. "Fire!"

Kapow! Jack was no more.

Willie played a sad melody on a broken fiddle, then blew mournful notes on a banged-up horn, while Tad beat a drum. They shuffled slowly by the White House in the funeral procession.

Tad dug a grave for Jack in Mrs. Lincoln's rose garden. Then Willie placed a single rose on Jack's coffin and shed a tear. Together, the boys were lowering Jack's coffin into the grave, when suddenly:

"Stop, there!" shouted Major Watt, the gardener, running furiously toward them. The boys' pet goat got so riled up she chased after the gardener. Major Watt stared at the big hole the boys had dug among the rosebushes, then glowered at Willie and Tad.

"Git! Git!" he shouted at them, waving his arms like he was shooing flies. The boys grabbed Jack's coffin and started running. "You set foot in that garden again, I'll put a hickory switch to your bottoms!"

A few minutes later, Willie and Tad stopped to catch their breath.

"Well, what do we do now?" Willie asked Tad. "We didn't give Jack a proper soldier's burial, so today doesn't really count. Tomorrow, we'll just have to start all over and shoot him again. If we shoot him, we gotta bury him. If we bury him, we gotta dig a hole in the garden, and Major Watt will have our hides!"

The boys sat on a log to think. They'd never been so stumped before. For once in their lives, they couldn't do just as they pleased.

Finally, Tad's face brightened.

"Who *says* we gotta shoot him?" Tad said, smiling. Tad had trouble pronouncing his *s*'es, so "shoot" sounded more like "thoot."

"Military regulations," said Willie. "You know the rules. Jack's done wrong. We don't got any choice, do we?"

"We'll get him a pardon," Tad said. "A pardon forgives a soldier forever."

"Who's gonna give it?" asked Willie.

"The Commander-in-Chief of the Army, of course!" Tad shouted.

Willie and Tad pounded up the White House stairs to the second-floor offices.
Mr. Nicolay tried to grab them as they flew by, but they were too quick for him.
The boys paraded into Mr. Lincoln's office and saluted like good soldiers.

Mr. Hay was talking with the president, but the children ignored him and plopped right down on the desk. He tugged nervously at his collar, muttering, "Not again."

"Well, my boys," said the president. "What can I do for you?"

"We need a pardon," Willie said.

"It's for Jack," Tad chimed in, taking the doll out of the box.

"I see," said the president. He crossed his arms over his chest. "It's not usual to grant pardons without a hearing. Tell me what Jack's done that he shouldn't have."

"Run away from a battle," said Willie.

"Another leg case, eh?" Mr. Lincoln chuckled. "Well, if a man's got a cowardly pair of legs, I reckon he can't help it. Anything else?"

"Fell asleep on picket duty," said Tad.

"Hmmm . . ." said Mr. Lincoln. "That's mighty serious. Anyone to speak for him besides you two scamps?"

Willie and Tad looked at each other and shrugged.

"No, Pa—sir," Willie said.

"Has he got any kinfolk? Brothers or sisters?"

"No, sir," the boys said together.

"Any friends?"

The boys shook their heads.

"No one likes Jack," said Tad.

"I'm not surprised," Mr. Hay said, frowning.

Mr. Lincoln clasped his big bony hands behind his back and paced the floor. He looked at his secretary with a question in his eyes. Mr. Hay shook his head.

Mr. Lincoln paused, then took a blank piece of paper from his desk drawer. "*I* will be his friend," he said, dipping his pen into the inkwell.

the doll Jack is pardoned
by order of the President

A Lincoln

The boys shouted, "Hurrah!" and waved the pardon in the air like a flag. Joining hands, they danced around their father, singing a song about "Old Abe Lincoln." Then they all fell, wrestling, to the floor. Tad and Willie laughed and tried to hold Mr. Lincoln down. Finally he broke free and stood up. The children galloped out and chased each other down the hall like frisky goats.

As Mr. Lincoln watched them go, the light seemed to go out of his eyes. He brushed off his long sleeves and sighed.

Mr. Lincoln picked up the doll Jack, which the boys had left behind.

"You know, John," he said to his secretary, "it makes me feel rested after a hard day's work, to find some good excuse to save a man's life."

The president put his arm around Mr. Hay's shoulder and tossed some papers into his tall stovepipe hat.

"Come on, John," he said, putting his hat on his head. "Jack and I will walk you home."

Author's Note

PRESIDENT LINCOLN really did write a pardon for his boys' soldier doll, Jack. The doll had been a gift to Tad, sent from the Sanitary Commission fair in New York. Here's how the real pardon came about:

Major Watt suggested to Tad and Willie that they seek a pardon for Jack. Mrs. Lincoln's young friend, Julia Taft, and Mr. Hay both tried to stop the boys (and their two playmates, Julia's younger brothers) before they bothered the busy president. When Mr. Lincoln heard Hay and the children arguing outside his office, he opened the door to ask what all the fuss was about. The president listened carefully to his youngest son's reply, then said, "Pardon for Jack, eh? You know, Tad, it's not usual to grant pardons without some sort of hearing. You come in here and tell me why you think Jack should have a pardon."

In her book *Tad Lincoln's Father*, published more than half a century later, Julia recalled that incident. According to Julia, after Tad argued briefly in Jack's defense, Mr. Lincoln replied, "Yes, Tad, I think you've made a case. It's a good law that no man shall twice be put in jeopardy of his life for the same offence, and you've already shot and buried Jack a dozen times. I guess he's entitled to a pardon."

Julia says that the president then wrote out a pardon for Tad, turned to his secretary, and said with a sigh, "I only wish, Hay, they were all that easy."

According to Julia, even after Jack was pardoned by the president, the boys put him on trial *again* and hanged him, for being "a spy."

For my story, I expanded Jack's hearing by modeling it after some of the actual informal pardon hearings that Lincoln held for real soldiers, as described in Carl Sandburg's biography of Lincoln. I hope that my version of Jack's "hearing" will help my readers see how Mr. Lincoln approached his real pardon cases. The president—who really once said that it made him feel rested after a hard day's work if he could find some good excuse for saving a man's life—looked for any legitimate reason to reverse soldiers' death sentences.

The pardon for Jack was not the only unusual one Lincoln granted. The Lincolns were given a live turkey as a present, intended for the First Family's Christmas dinner. When the time came for it to be killed, young Tad started crying and begged his father to pardon the turkey. Lincoln obliged, thus sparing the bird's life—it became a White House pet—and starting what eventually developed into a presidential Thanksgiving tradition that continues to this day.

OUR CAST OF CHARACTERS

ABRAHAM AND MARY LINCOLN'S CHILDREN

Willie (William Wallace) Lincoln was born December 21, 1850. Bright and sweet-tempered, Willie was, many people said, the Lincoln child most like his father. He enjoyed writing poetry and memorizing train timetables.

Willie died in the White House on February 20, 1862, at the age of eleven. He succumbed to "bilious fever"—probably what we'd call typhoid fever, today—which may have been caused by pollution in the White House's drinking water.

Thomas ("Tad") Lincoln was born April 4, 1853. Tad had a speech impediment—which means that he had difficulty speaking clearly—possibly because of a partially cleft palate. His father nicknamed him "tadpole," because as a baby Tad had a large head and small body. When Tad was a young boy, he was known for his clever pranks and mischief. Tad died of either tuberculosis or pneumonia in 1871.

The Lincolns had two other sons: Edward, who died in 1850 at the age of three, before Mr. Lincoln became president; and their oldest son, Robert Todd Lincoln, who lived to the ripe old age of eighty-two. Robert was away at Harvard College at the time this story takes place, and later served as a Union Army captain in the war.

JULIA TAFT BAYNE

Julia Taft (1845–1933) was sixteen years old at the time this story takes place. The daughter of the chief examiner at the U.S. Patent office, she was a family friend of the Lincolns whose little brothers, Bud and Holly, often played with Tad and Willie. Julia was with the First Family so often that she became like a nanny to the Lincoln boys—and almost like a daughter to Mr. and Mrs. Lincoln, who never had (but always wanted) a daughter of their own. The president teasingly called her a "flibbertigibbet," which he said meant "a small, slim thing with curls and a white dress and a blue sash who flies instead of walking."

JOHN HAY AND JOHN NICOLAY

John Hay (1838–1905) was only twenty-three years old when he became Mr. Lincoln's White House secretary. Hay and the president's other secretary, John Nicolay (1832–1901), lived in the White House, across the hall from Lincoln's office. In my story, Mr. Lincoln was joking when he offered to walk Hay home.

Hay and Nicolay were the president's close, loyal friends. Behind Mr. Lincoln's back they called him "the old man," "the tycoon," "the chief," or "the ancient," but this was all in fun. Hay went on to become ambassador to Great Britain and secretary of state under President Theodore Roosevelt. Nicolay became a diplomat, and later a marshal to the U.S. Supreme Court. The two men also wrote a ten-volume biography of President Lincoln.

ABRAHAM LINCOLN

Born into poverty in Kentucky in 1809, Abraham Lincoln became the sixteenth president of the United States. He successfully led this country through a Civil War (1861–1865) that cost over half a million American soldiers' lives but preserved the Union of states and its democratic form of government. In 1862, he signed the Emancipation Proclamation, which ordered that any slaves in states still in rebellion against the United States government by January 1, 1863, would be "then, thenceforward, and forever free." All the slaves in the United States were later freed and granted full citizenship by the thirteenth and fourteenth amendments to the U.S. Constitution, ratified in 1865 and 1868.

On April 9, 1865, the main army of the rebellious South (Confederate States of America) surrendered to Union General Ulysses S. Grant. The war was almost over, and victory for the North was now certain. Five days later, Abraham Lincoln was shot by a Confederate sympathizer, actor John Wilkes Booth, while he and his wife, Mary, were watching a play, *Our American Cousin*, at Ford's Theatre in Washington, D.C. President Lincoln died the next morning.

Mary Lincoln (1818–1882) outlived her husband and three of her four sons. She never fully recovered from the tragic events of her life.

The two hundredth anniversary of Abraham Lincoln's birth will be celebrated on February 12, 2009.

Resources for Learning More about Abraham Lincoln and His Family

There are many Lincoln-related historic sites and museums in the United States. Here are just a few places where you can learn more about Mr. and Mrs. Lincoln and their boys:

Abraham Lincoln Presidential Library and Museum, http://www.alplm.org/home.html
112 North Sixth Street, Springfield, Illinois, 62701

Lincoln Home National Historic Site, http://www.nps.gov/liho/index.htm
413 South Eighth Street, Springfield, Illinois, 62701

Ford's Theatre National Historic Site, http://www.fordstheatre.org/
511 10th Street NW, Washington, D.C., 20004

Lincoln's New Salem State Historic Site, http://www.lincolnsnewsalem.com
15588 History Lane, Petersburg, Illinois, 62675

Abraham Lincoln Birthplace National Historic Site, http://www.nps.gov/abli/
2995 Lincoln Farm Road, Hodgenville, Kentucky, 42748

Abraham Lincoln Online, http://showcase.netins.net/web/creative/lincoln.html

Mr. Lincoln's White House, http://www.mrlincolnswhitehouse.org

Abraham Lincoln's Historical Digitization Project, http://lincoln.lib.niu.edu

Lincoln Bicentennial Web site, http://www.lincolnbicentennial.gov

Selected Bibliography:

Tad Lincoln's Father by Julia Taft Bayne, with an introduction by Mary A. Decredico. Reprint, University of Nebraska Press, 2001.

Lincoln by David Herbert Donald. Simon & Schuster, 1995.

Lincoln: A Photobiography by Russell Freedman. Clarion Books, 1987.

Team of Rivals: The Political Genius of Abraham Lincoln by Doris Kearns Goodwin. Simon & Schuster, 2005.

War, Terrible War 1855–1865 (Vol. 6 of *The Story of US*) by Joy Hakim. Oxford University Press, second edition, 1999.

Lincoln at Cooper Union: The Speech That Made Abraham Lincoln President by Harold Holzer. Simon & Schuster, 2004.

Lincoln: A Picture Story of His Life by Stefan Lorant. Revised and enlarged edition, W. W. Norton, 1969.

With Malice Toward None: A Life of Abraham Lincoln by Stephen B. Oates. Reprint, Harper Perennial, 1994.

The Lincolns in the White House: Four Years That Shattered a Family by Jerrold M. Packard. St. Martin's Press, 2005.

Lincoln's Sons by Ruth Painter Randall. Little, Brown, 1955.

Abraham Lincoln: The Prairie Years and The War Years by Carl Sandburg. Reprint, Harvest Books, 2002.

Manhunt: The 12-Day Chase for Lincoln's Killer by James L. Swanson. Morrow, 2006.

For further information on the Civil War, read books by Shelby Foote, James McPherson, and Bruce Catton, or see Ken Burns's PBS-TV series *The Civil War*.